Jacob of Sarug's Homily on the Entrance of Our Lord into Sheol

Texts from Christian Late Antiquity

82

Series Editor

George Anton Kiraz

TeCLA (Texts from Christian Late Antiquity) is a series presenting ancient Christian texts both in their original languages and with accompanying contemporary English translations.

Jacob of Sarug's Homily on the Entrance of Our Lord into Sheol

Edited and Translated by
Daniel L. McConaughy

Text Edition by
Roger Akhrass
Imad Syryany

2024

Gorgias Press LLC, 954 River Road, Piscataway, NJ, 08854, USA

www.gorgiaspress.com

Copyright © 2024 by Gorgias Press LLC

All rights reserved under International and Pan-American Copyright Conventions. No part of this publication may be reproduced, stored in a retrieval system or transmitted in any form or by any means, electronic, mechanical, photocopying, recording, scanning or otherwise without the prior written permission of Gorgias Press LLC.

2024

ISBN		ISSN 1935-6846
Hardback	978-1-4632-4815-4	
eBook	978-1-4632-4816-1	

Library of Congress Cataloging-in-Publication Data

A Cataloging-in-Publication Record is available at the Library of Congress.

Printed in the United States of America

TABLE OF CONTENTS

Acknowledgements vii
Introduction 1
   Overview 1
   Author 1
   Title 3
   Opening Prayer... 4
   Important Themes 6
      Gates/Bars of Sheol 6
      Death and Sheol 7
      Comparisons with Jonah and the Patriarch
         Jacob 8
      Christ's Victory.. 9
   Conclusion.. 10
   Sources of the Syriac Text 11
   Translation Style 11
   Outline of the Homily 12
Text and Translation 15
   Opening Prayer... 16
   The Crucifixion... 22
   Sheol the Devourer... 24
   Death the Dominator... 26
   Death, the Victorious King 34
   Enoch Alone Escaped from Death 36
   Plea to the Hearer 40
   The Battle of Our Lord Prior to Entering Sheol 40
   The Lord's Vision of Sheol... 46
   The Incarnation 48

    The Lord's Journey in Sheol 50
    Comparison with Jonah 54
    The Dead One Gives Life 56
    Comparison with the Patriarch Jacob 58
    Christ's Death and the Overthrow of Sheol 60
    Conclusion 66
Bibliography 69
Index 71
    Topical Index 71
    Index of Scriptural Allusions 73

ACKNOWLEDGEMENTS

The author would like to thank Archbishop Roger Akhrass and Imad Syryany for their permission to use their critical text and apparatus in this translation edition. In addition, Archbishop Akhrass assisted the author in clarifying a few Syriac texts during the initial translation work. Prof. Sebastian Brock kindly reviewed the complete translation and provided many helpful comments and corrections, and the author is most thankful for his sharing of his time and expertise. The author would also like to thank Fr. Dr. Jacob Thekeparambil, Director of the St. Ephrem Ecumenical Institute in Kerala, for introducing him to Mor Jacob's *mimre*.

INTRODUCTION

OVERVIEW

This *mimro* (a metrical homily) sets forth with great effectiveness how Christ gave His life and entered into Sheol like any other dead human so that He might conquer it. It is composed of 374 lines in Jacob of Serugh's well known twelve-syllable-per-line meter.

With matchless imagery Jacob impresses on the reader the domination of Death and Sheol over mankind and the utter helplessness of the human race. He tells how Enoch was the only human who escaped Sheol. To develop the homily, he uses the types of Jonah and the patriarch Jacob. He tells of the necessity of Christ's death that allowed Him to enter Sheol as any other dead human, but His power over life allowed Him to trick and destroy Sheol and Death and liberate the dead.

AUTHOR

Jacob of Serugh (d. 521) has long been known as the 'Flute of the Holy Spirit and the Harp of the Church.' He even refers to himself in this way in his *Second Mimro Concerning the Praise of the Morning*:

1. May Your love stir me as a breath stirs the pipe, O Son of God,
   And may I sing Your praise richly.
2. I am Your flute, command me – I shall give as for your praise,
   Simple words full of the wonders of your workmanship.

3. Breath in me, O my Master, as with an empty pipe,
And I will sing every praise with great wonder distinctly…
7. I am a harp with members like with strings,
The gesture of Your creative power 'strung' me when it fitted me,
9. O Lord, let not the vessel which Your workmanship devised, be silent,
But by Your spirit stir its talkative strings…
11. The breath puts a sound within the flute,
And the finger which strums, stirs the music from the harp.[1]

Mor Jacob was one of the most prolific Syriac writers of the early Syriac church, second to Ephrem (d. 373). 763 homilies are ascribed to him. Bedjan's five-volume work[2] contains 195 homilies, and Akhrass and Syryany's two-volume work[3] contains another 160 homilies. A member of the Syriac Orthodox Church, he was a Miaphysite, rejecting Chalcedon, but was not as active in the Christological disagreements of the time as his contemporary colleague, Philoxenus. This characteristic broadened the audience of readers of his mimre. His homilies were very popular, being translated into Armenian, Arabic, Ethiopic (by way of Arabic) and Georgian. The oldest manuscripts date from the 6th century and several later manuscripts from the 11th to the 13th centuries contain collections of more than 200 mimre.[4]

---

[1] Roger Akhrass and Imad Syryany, *160 Unpublished Homilies of Jacob of Serugh*, 2 vols., Damascus: Department of Syriac Studies – Syriac Orthodox Patriarchate, 2017, vol. 1, p. 468. The author and Fr. Dr. Jacob Thekeparampil are preparing translations of Mor Jacob's mimre on the liturgical hours of *Sapro*, *Ramsho* and *Lilyo* (forthcoming).

[2] Paul Bedjan, *Homiliae Selectae Mar-Jacobi Sarugensis*, I–V, Lipzig: Otto Harrassowitz (1905–10). This has been reprinted more recently by Gorgias Press, 2006 along with 11 other homilies.

[3] Op. cit. Akhrass and Syryany.

[4] Sebastian Brock, "Yaʿqub of Serugh (ca. 451–521) [Syr. Orth.]," *Gorgias Encyclopedic Dictionary of the Syriac Heritage Electronic Edition*: https://gedsh.bethmardutho.org/entry/Yaqub-of-Serugh.

INTRODUCTION

Mor Jacob was born in Kurtam on the Euphrates in the eastern Roman Empire ca. 451. By the early sixth century, he was a chorepiscopus of Ḥawra, and by 519, he was a bishop of Baṭnan, a city in the district of Serugh, southwest of Edessa, in what is now in Türkiye near the border of Syria.

TITLE

The title, "The Entrance of Our Lord into Sheol," is notable in that it does not say "Descent," a more frequently occurring term relating to this subject. As one reads the homily, it is clear that "entrance" is in the sense of a triumphal or formal entrance into that place of misery.[5] (Since this word in English is unclear, 'entrance' is not a portal or a door of some type.) The word, "descent," ܡܚܬܬܐ, nevertheless, does occur in the homily in lines 298 and 343. In lines 297–298, Christ's "entrance," ܡܥܠܬܐ, is compared to Jonah's "descent" into the sea:

> His entrance within the grave also resembled,
> that descent of the son of the Hebrews within the sea.

In lines 343–344, we read:

> Through the descent of our Lord, this peace was in Sheol itself,
> and praise resounded in the desolate place of the house of
> the departed ones.

"Entrance" occurs three times: lines 135, 187 and 297. The third was just discussed above. The second, at line 187, refers to the title:

> "Concerning the Entrance of our Lord to Sheol," I have begun to speak…

---

[5] See op. cit. Bedjan, Vol. 5, pp. 613–31 for the same word used in the title of homily 174: "The Entrance of Our Lord into the Temple," ܡܥܠܬܗ ܕܡܪܢ ܠܗܝܟܠܐ.

The first use of occurs at line 135, where it is used with its antonym, "departure." It is translated here as, "entering."

> The command went out concerning entering within the grave,
> but [concerning] the departure, no one was able to speak about that.

Though "descent," ܡܚܬܬܐ, is not used in the title nor frequently, the cognate verb, "descend," ܢܚܬ, occurs 19 times in lines: 59, 61, 64, 81, 84, 122, 230, 256, 295, 307, 313, 319, 324, 325, 326, 328, 338, 345, and 358. This verb is often associated with the grave and Sheol; so the 'descent – idea' is in the text. Thus, the major emphasis of the homily, indicated by the title, is the 'entrance', not the 'descent,' namely a triumphal or formal entrance of the Lord into Sheol.[6]

OPENING PRAYER

Mor Jacob opens his *mimre* with a prayer.[7] This opening prayer is 44 lines long, more than 10% of the total. Perhaps this reflects the difficulty of the subject for him. Line 1 addresses Christ as "Radiance," ܨܡܚܐ. This word is used only once in the New Testament Peshitta, in Hebrews 1:3, where it refers to Christ as the radiance of God's glory. Line 2 begins with a favorite word form of Jacob's which is frequently found at the beginning and throughout his works. Here, it is the aphel form of ܕܢܚ, "make to dawn," which is followed by the cognate noun, ܕܢܚܐ, "dawn." Both ܨܡܚܐ and ܕܢܚܐ are examined in detail by Akhrass and McConaughy.[8] These words are highlighted in the opening four lines:

> O **Radiance** by Whose <u>flashes</u> the depths of Sheol were lit up,

---

[6] It should be kept in mind that the 'entrance' is a result of a 'descent.'
[7] I am unaware of any mimre that do not open with a prayer.
[8] Severios Roger Akhrass and Daniel L. McConaughy, "Ṣemaḥ, Anatole, and Denḥa: Translation and Evolution of a Messianic Title," *Syriac Orthodox Patriarchal Journal* 60 (2022), pp. 1–18.

> Make the light from Your instruction **dawn** on my thoughts.
> O New Sun who shed abroad Its **dawn** on the land of the dead,
> Enlighten my mind with Your ideas so that I might recount Your beauty...

This opening is remarkably similar to the opening of another mimro, *Concerning the Star that Appeared to the Magi*:

> 1. O Great **Dawn** Who fills the world with your <u>rays</u>:
>   **Make** Your light **dawn** upon my thoughts ...
> 2. O **Radiance** of the Father who sheds light on those in darkness...[9]

The similarity in the openings of the two prayers extends beyond ܪܘܡܚܐ and ܕܢܚ. In line 1, "flashes" is ܙܠܝܩܐ, and is the same word as "rays" in line 1 of *Concerning the Star that Appeared to the Magi*.

Jacob asks Christ to subdue his mind so that he might proceed with the homily, in lines 9–10:

> O King who has broken down rebellious strongholds by Your courage,
> Settle upon my mind so that it might work for Your Dominion.

In lines 17–20, Jacob likens his mind to Sheol, where he calls it a "foul sanctuary" and "vile place":

> Summon Freewill, which guards the gates, to lift up their bars,
> And enter and dwell in that foul sanctuary and it will be sanctified by You.
> You will not eschew from entering the vile place,
> For a grave, too, the sight of which is hateful, became Your lodging...

---

[9] Op. cit. Bedjan, vol. 1, p. 84. A translation of this homily by Daniel McConaughy and Jacob Thekeparampil is forthcoming: *The Homily of Mor Jacob Concerning the Star that Appeared to the Magi*, Awṣar Ṣlawoto 11, Kottayam: SEERI, 2024.

He continues to develop his request for Christ to dwell in his mind so that he might bring forth a *mimro* to His victory in lines 37–38:

> My mind covered up Your teaching by its rebellion,
> Subdue it so that it would break forth [and] proceed [and]
> give what is within it.

IMPORTANT THEMES

Gates/Bars of Sheol

The Gates/Bars of Sheol figure often in this homily. Though Jacob mentions the Diatessaronic term "bars," ܡܘܟܠܐ, he does so only twice, an in each instance, with "door"/ "gate." In lines 17–18, he prays that God would work in his mind:

> Summon Freewill, which guards the gates, to lift up their bars,
> and enter and dwell in that foul sanctuary and it will be
> sanctified by you.

In lines 351–352 referring to *Sheol*, we see the same imagery of door and bars:

> Humbly did He enter through the door all by Himself,
> so that He might free the prisoners and take the bars [of
> Sheol] and bring out the people.

"Door(s)," ܬܪܥܐ, is used much more frequently than "bars." "Door(s)" occurs 15 times in lines: 12, 17, 73, 89, 116, 129, 139, 233, 245, 258, 273, 278, 346, 351, and 353. The context is usually *Sheol*. The phrase "doors of *Sheol*" occurs at lines 89, 245, 273, and 346. Based on this, we can conclude that Jacob prefers "doors" over "bars" in the imagery of *Sheol*.

Sebastian Brock's important article, "The Gates/Bars of Sheol Revisited,"[10] deserves a mention here for anyone who

---

[10] Sebastian P. Brock, "The Gates/Bars of Sheol Revisited," *Sayings of Jesus: Canonical and Non-canonical: Essays in Honour of T.Baarda*, ed. By

wants to pursue a study of these important words. This article provides a thorough treatment of the use of gates and bars in the context of the Old Testament, Syriac patristics and the Diatessaron.

Death and Sheol

Death and Sheol are used frequently throughout the *mimro*. Death occurs 44 times and Sheol occurs 23 times. Jacob describes Death and Sheol in very striking terms:

69. Sheol the devourer, the abyss that laid hold on all generations,
70. the fortress that no one from the dwellers of the earth ever subdued.
73. The doors are open before the entrants and they are not shut...
95. Mothers were giving birth to it up to Jesus,
96. its name attached itself from within the womb to all the infants.
97. It took captive creation and designated it [to be] its own and it ruled on the earth,
98. it took their infants [as] tribute [right] from the wombs.
99. The crowns from all the nations, thousands of the dead, came to it,
100. families approached and worshipped it with their corpses...
107. Lamentations went forth like 'eulogies' concerning its power...
123. It did not condescend to capture [mere] possessions with its bow,
124. but only over the possessors did it vaunt itself.
125. It despised gold and subdued the lords of riches in its habitation,

---

W. L. Peterson, J.S, Vos and H. J. de Jong, Supplements to Novum Testamentum, vol. 89 (1997), 7–24.

126. instead of properties, it took property owners to be its
        bread...
131. Everyone coming [into the world] was considered to be a
        return to Sheol...
141. What city is there that prospered so much as Sheol,
142. which became rich with harvests without costs?

Only Enoch escaped death, and barely at that:

169. His Lord gave him a hand and He translated him mercifully
        to Eden,
170. lest he meet with death and it lay hold of him like the rest...
181. He had fled by himself, no others did he lead with himself,
182. and without companions, he alone escaped.

Sheol was invincible as we read in lines 239-244:

> Moses the deliverer rose up in Egypt and lead out the People,
> yet he was unable to lead out Sheol's prisoners.
> Joshua had overthrown high walls and slaughtered kings,
> but when he had entered the city of death, he did not depart
>   from it.
> Furthermore, David had killed that mighty warrior of the
>   Philistines,
> he was illustrious in battle, yet death imprisoned him just
>   like his companions.

All the great champions were vanquished by Sheol.

Comparisons with Jonah and the Patriarch Jacob

Jonah is a popular figure in the Syriac Church as a type of Christ. Above we discussed the use of "entrance" and "descent" in lines 297–298 and will not repeat it. The discussion of Jonah is introduced and concluded with:

295. He had descended to the depth like Bar Mattai to the bottom
        of the sea,
296. And death received Him like the great fish [received] Jonah...
305. Our Lord had given this sign to the sons of His People,
306. And it suffices to persuade [them] that even his mortality

was vitality.

With regard to the patriarch Jacob, the comparison Mor Jacob employs is less well known than Jonah's. It is presented as an extended comparison where Jacob sleeping with his staff is like Christ dying on the Cross. Because angels visit Jacob, a symbol of Christ, how much more would they visit and attend to Christ Himself:

323. Jacob had slept on the top of the mountain as he depicted it,
324. And the host of heaven descended to him with great praise.
325. And if it happened that the angels descended to where the
    servant slept,
326. How much more would they have descended to where their
    Lord had slept?...
333. He was crucified in his sleep, as if in death, with a staff in
    his hand,
334. He had depicted there exactly the crucifixion of the Son...
337. The watchers honored the foreshadowing of the Son of God,
338. The angels descended because of the symbol they saw there.
339. And if there was honor for the exalted ones for the figure,
340. [then] the hosts [of heaven] were insignificant [compared]
    to the True One Himself.

The above are a sampling of the detailed comparison of Jacob as a type of Christ.

Christ's Victory

Christ's victory over Sheol is described at length. The following is a sample from lines 347–351 and 359:

> The city of strength that had not been subdued by mighty
>   warriors,
> Into it the Slain One entered and He broke it down suddenly
>   and it became a laughing stock.
> The King is asleep yet the fortress which is more rebellious
>   than any is subdued,
> He was bound in sleep yet He freed the prisoners so that
>   they would go out with Him.
> Humbly did he enter through the door all by Himself...

> He had plunged into death so that from within the depth He
> might draw up our race…

Line 359 ties the death to baptism, like St. Paul in Romans 6:3–4. "Plunged" is ܥܡܕ, the root of the various words for "baptism" and "baptize." Jacob of Serug provides an in-depth treatment of Christ's accomplishments over death and Sheol by discussing what He would not have accomplished had he listened to Simon and not gone to Golgotha in his homily, "On Simon Kepha when Our Lord Said "Get Behind Me Satan.""[11]

CONCLUSION

The closing lines 363–366 provide a brilliant rhetorical flourish. They are translated in a way to show their structure:

> He entered the garners which are only touched in death,
> > He had travelled in the place that none but the slain
> > > [can] see it.
> > He had lodged in the place that none but the buried
> > > [can] dwell in it,
> He entered the ambushes that are experienced by none but the dead.

An examination of this Syriac text shows very tightly structured and nuanced grammatical constructions in chiastic form. The reader should consult the text and notes to the translation below for the grammatical details. The direct translation above, shows some of the structure of Mor Jacob's Syriac. The first and fourth lines begin with "He entered" and end with "in death" and "the dead," respectively. The middle second and third lines are very similarly structured to one another as shown. The Syriac translated by "only" and "none but" is very skillfully executed using

---

[11] Jacob Thekeparambil and Daniel McConaughy, *Jacob of Serugh's Three Mimre on Simon Peter: 1. On the Question of our Lord and the Revelation Simon Received from the Father, 2. On Simon Kepha When Our Lord Said "Get Behind Me Satan," 3. On the Denial of Simon, Awṣar Ṣlawoto* 10, Kottayam: SEERI, 2023, stanzas 142–168, pp. 174–184.

the same construction. This displays Jacob's tremendous rhetorical and compositional skill using the 12-syllable line. To hear him read it would have been an unforgettable experience.

SOURCES OF THE SYRIAC TEXT

Severios Roger Akhrass and Imad Syryany kindly allowed the translator to include the Syriac text from their monumental work, *160 Unpublished Homilies of Jacob of Serugh*.[12] This massive two-volume work rests upon the collations of many manuscripts and provides a critical text with an apparatus of variant readings. *The Entrance of Our Lord into Sheol* is found on pages 184-191 of Volume 1.

The base manuscript for *The Entrance of Our Lord into Sheol* is Damascus 12/13 written A.D. 1031.

The manuscripts used in the apparatus for this mimro are:

Manuscripts of the Syriac Orthodox Patriarchate, Damascus
B – Dam. 12/14 (11th cent.)
C – Dam. 12/15 (donated 1156)

Manuscripts of the Church of the Forty Martyrs, Mardin
(digitized by Hill Museum and Manuscript Library)
M – CFMM 130 (12th/13th cent.)
M_5 – CFMM 135 (?)

Manuscripts of the St. Thomas Church, Mosul
P – STC 74 (13th cent.)

Vatican Library
V – Vat. Syr. 118 (1121)

TRANSLATION STYLE

The translation almost always follows the text as presented in the main section. Occasionally, variant readings are translated when they seem clearer. These exceptions are noted.

---

[12] Op. cit.

Translation style, depending on the translator's taste, can range from the literal direct rendering of the Syriac, resulting in a less idiomatic English, to a dynamic equivalency or even a paraphrase that may result in a more idiomatic modern English but somewhat hides the underlying Syriac idiom. The translation herein attempts to follow the underlying Syriac original in a more direct way, as closely as English permits without being overly unidiomatic. Sometimes more literal renderings are in the footnotes. Added words are put in brackets to make the translation clearer to the reader.

The translation unit is generally the 12-syllable line, though sometimes the two-line stanza is the unit when the English requires it. At times, the translation unit may expand to aid the reader in understanding the antecedents. For instance, "death" is masculine and "Sheol" is feminine, and the gender of the pronominal suffix or gender of the verb provides the clue regarding which antecedent is intended. In some cases, footnotes are provided to direct the reader. Every attempt has been made to translate consistently throughout the homily. It is hoped that this translation approach will assist the reader who wishes to follow the Syriac text. Many of the footnotes to the translation provide help for the reader of the Syriac because the rhetorical style of Jacob of Serugh can sometimes be difficult to follow and the many word plays are not always translatable.

There are not a lot of Biblical citations in this homily. Jacob uses Biblical terminology and provides many allusions. The footnotes indicate allusions to Scripture.

OUTLINE OF THE HOMILY

This outline provides a guide to the reader since Mor Jacob did not provide section headings. Because he does not always follow a rigorous, logical progression, outlining the mimro is somewhat subjective. Another reader may outline the mimro differently. Nevertheless, the main topics are identified by line numbers.

1–44	Opening Prayer
45–68	The Crucifixion
69–84	Sheol the Devourer

INTRODUCTION

85–156	Death the Dominator
157–182	Enoch Alone Escaped from Death
183–186	Plea to the Hearer
187–224	The Battle of our Lord Prior to Entering Sheol
225–250	The Lord's Vision of Sheol
251–262	The Incarnation
263–294	The Lord's Journey in Sheol
295–306	Comparison with Jonah
307–322	The Dead One Gives Life
323–342	Comparison with the Patriarch Jacob
343–370	Christ's Death and the Overthrow of Sheol
371–374	Conclusion

TEXT AND TRANSLATION

HOLY MOR JACOB'S HOMILY ON THE ENTRANCE OF OUR LORD INTO SHEOL

OPENING PRAYER

1 O Radiance[1] by Whose flashes the depths of Sheol were lit up,
    make the light from Your[2] instruction dawn[3] on my thoughts.
    O New Sun who shed abroad Its[4] dawn on the land of the dead,
    enlighten my mind with Your ideas so that I might recount Your beauty.
5 O Immortal One who died on the cross to restore us,
    allow me[5] to become dead to the world[6] so that I might live to You, O my Lord.
    O living Murdered One by whose mortality You distributed[7] life,
    by the life that is from You, 'murder'[8] the sin which lurks in me.
    O King who has broken down rebellious strongholds by Your[9] courage,

---

[1] Heb. 1:3 contains the only NT use of this word: "[the Son] is the radiance of [God's] glory…"

[2] BM₅V

[3] Jacob is fond of using ܕܢܚ and its cognates. See lines 3–4. For a detailed study of this word, see Jacob Thekeparambil and Daniel McConaughy, "The Star and the Magi in Jacob of Serugh and the Early Syriac Tradition," *Syriac Orthodox Patriarchal Journal* 59, (2021), pp. 41–54.

[4] In Syriac, third person singular to agree with the vocative subject. A feature of Jacob's opening prayers. See especially lines 9–10.

[5] Lit. "give to me."

[6] Cf. Col. 2:20.

[7] In Syriac, third person singular to agree with the vocative subject.

[8] Note the word play of "Murdered One" and "murder."

[9] In Syriac, third person singular to agree with the subject. Note the second person pronominal suffix in the second line of this stanza.

---

¹⁰ BM₅V title ܡܶܠܬܳܐ ܕܡܳܪܢ ܡܳܪܝ ܝܥܩܘܒ ܡܠܦܢܐ ܕܥܠ ܡܪܟܒܬܗ ܕܓܠܝ ܚܙܩܝܐܠ
¹¹ M ܘܒܥܛܡܗ
¹² BM₅V ܘܠܐܩܝܢ
¹³ B ܗܘܡܬܝܝ
¹⁴ BCMM₅V ܟܰܣܢܝ̈
¹⁵ M ܘܢܶܫܡܥ

10   settle upon my mind so that it might work[16] for Your Dominion.
Until You have subdued it, O my Lord, do not depart lest it rebel,
be patient with it so that the door would open and Your suffering would enter.
Do not become weary and turn away; it [the mind][17] cannot resist You,
the Evil one is [trying to] grasp it, therefore it delayed coming to You.

15   Shoot an arrow at the Caluminator so that he will flee from it,[18]
and that I may easily again return[19] to Your dwelling.
Summon Freewill, which guards the gates,[20] to lift up their bars,[21]
and enter and dwell in that foul sanctuary and it will be sanctified by You.
You will not eschew from entering the vile place,

20   for a grave, too, the sight of which is hateful, became Your lodging.
Your kingdom broke open the house of the departed, and how then,
can it shrink from the house of my mind because of my debts?[22]
Enter, O Mighty One, and drive them from their dwellings,
and they will not delay there when they see You.

---

[16] Lit. "give a hand to."
[17] i.e., the mind in line 10.
[18] i.e., the mind.
[19] ܘܐܘܦܝ - ms. M.
[20] Plural – ms. M.
[21] ܡܘܟܠܬܐ – cf. "bars of Sheol." See Sebastian P. Brock, "The Gates/Bars of Sheol Revisited," *Sayings of Jesus: Canonical and Non-canonical: Essays in Honour of T.Baarda*, ed. By W. L. Peterson, J.S, Vos and H. J. de Jong, Supplements to Novum Testamentum, vol. 89 (1997) 7–24.
[22] "Debts," in the sense of "sins." See Mt. 6:12.

---

23 B
24 V
25 CMM₅V
26 M
27 M
28 M
29 B
30 B ; M
31 M
32 M
33 B ; CM₅V ; M
34 M
35 C
36 M
37 M
38 M₅

25 The city of my mind was plotting to rebel from You,
    may the awesome ranks come to let loose Your suffering upon it.
    Call to the legions of Your ideas[40] and let them surround it,
    and may voices go out from among the ranks and stir it up.
    Rain the arrows of Your love upon it from every side,
30 while it is being pierced by the commandments which Your love sharpened.
    Lift up and encompass it with the polished armor of faith,
    and may the hidden mysteries become ambushes and surround it.
    Stand up, O Instruction, like a steward and incite Your people,
    so that it would strive with the fortified village that had disregarded its Lord.
35 O Living Cross that broke through the walls that had been strong,
    stay with me [so that] I might desire that You enter to be victorious even in me.
    My mind covered up Your teaching by its rebellion.
    Subdue it so that it would break forth [and] proceed [and] give what is within it.
    And whether it wants to or not, You will not let it go.
40 Place in it your banner so that it might be stirred by Your victory.
    May the sign of Your suffering be shown to it from every side,

---

[39] MV ܢܗܘܘܢ

[40] Cf. line 4.

---

⁴¹ B ; CM₅ ; MV
⁴² M
⁴³ CMM₅V
⁴⁴ B
⁴⁵ M
⁴⁶ CMM₅V
⁴⁷ BMV
⁴⁸ B
⁴⁹ B ; CMM₅V
⁵⁰ CMM₅V
⁵¹ BV
⁵² M₅
⁵³ B

and depict the image of Your death on its walls [so that] it will
    be adorned by You.
Behold the world is subdued beneath Your victory and is subject
    to You,
and underneath Your heel the officials of all dominions are laid.

THE CRUCIFIXION

45　Who is the well-known King who is crucified naked,
and the deaf [and dumb] elements are reeling from Him silently?
He cried out on the cross and the wicked one fell from his power,
He shouted at death and it rose with trembling within Sheol.
He was triumphant in death and made His way straight to the
    house of the departed,
50　He made suffering suffer and He killed death and He reigned
    over all.
He had opened His mouth and drank the cup[55] which death gave
    Him,
and He, in turn, made [death] drink[56] the cup of suffering which
    it mixed for Him.
Death had rendered double with its taste[57] of suffering that the
    Messiah suffered,
Because the cup which it mixed was not as bitter as that which
    He drank.
55　It went forth to smite and He was wounded mightily,
it shot an arrow, and it (arrow) turned around [and] swiftly
    ripped it (Death) open.
It overthrew the King and it fell from His dominion,

---

[54] B ܚܢܝܼܟ
[55] Mt. 26:39,42.
[56] Aph.
[57] BMg has "the cup."

---

⁵⁸ MM₅
⁵⁹ B
⁶⁰ B
⁶¹ BM₅
⁶² BM₅
⁶³ CMV

it struck the Strong Man and as it was falling, He laid it beneath Himself.
He was hung up on the mountain and He descended, He subdued it at the bottom of its hole,
60 He suffered on the cross and He had not been able to rescue Himself.
It rushed upon the Stone, the Head of the building, that it might bring Him[64] down to its hole,
and turning to Him,[65] He[66] had ground it to pieces soundly.[67]
They rolled away the stone so that they might set It[68] in the building of the dead,
and as It was going down, It broke down the very walls of Sheol.
65 They cut down the Cedar1 so that It would fall on the earth and Its story would come to an end,
but It rose up to bear the burden of the world on Its rafters.
Who indeed has seen a king killed by [his] pursuers,
and [then] his corpse enters to subdue the walled city which rebelled against him?

SHEOL THE DEVOURER

Sheol the devourer, the abyss that laid hold on all generations,
70 the fortress that no one from the dwellers of the earth ever subdued.
The city which gathered up all nations yet was not filled up,[69]
and as many as enter, its womb holds them because it[70] will suffice for them.
The doors are open before the entrants and they are not shut,

---

[64] Fem. to agree with fem. noun, "stone."
[65] i.e., the Stone (fem. in Syriac).
[66] i.e., "the Stone."
[67] BCMM₅V reads, "by His (fem., agreeing with fem. gender of ܟܐܦܐ) soundness."
[68] i.e., "the Stone."
[69] This reflects the imagery of Hab. 2:5 and Prov. 30:15–16.
[70] i.e., "the city."

---

[71] M₅

[72] BCMM₅V

[73] MM₅V

[74] MV

[75] M₅

[76] CMM₅V

       and no foot stirs to get out of its abode.
75   Death goes out, plundering the dead of all generations,
       and it brings in [and] gathers [them] up in a stronghold that no one has [ever] subdued.
       The arms of Sheol had been spread widely to lay hold of the dead,
       its paths empty into its dwelling places from all sides.
       The courageous entered and the lords of the nations struggled with it,
80   the strong ones fell and even the mighty became cowards.
       The brave went down to it and the race ceased from the swift,
       the lords of the army were abased by it and became dung.
       Generations entered and the ages of their successions came to an end,
       and families went down and the history of their genealogies[77] vanished.

DEATH THE DOMINATOR

85   There was a wine press, and in it death trod on all the rulers,
       it overthrew crowns, it seized the territories, it scattered the proud.
       It set its heel above the head of the exalted kings,
       it stomped on and laughed at the statures of all the strong ones.
       And it bowed down and brought the high cedars into the doors of Sheol,

---

[77] Lit. "history of their births."

Text and Translation

---

⁷⁸ CMM₅V
⁷⁹ V
⁸⁰ B
⁸¹ MM₅V
⁸² B
⁸³ M₅
⁸⁴ B M;
⁸⁵ V one page om.
⁸⁶ B
⁸⁷ B

90	it cut down and threw down the upright palm trees with the destruction[88] of its fire.
	It fell upon the forest of men to hew [them] down,
	it utterly destroyed and cast even the chosen into the bosom of its fire.
	It cut down Adam, the head of the cedars of every field,
	and indeed it exalts itself over the tree tops that came out from him.[89]
95	Mothers were giving birth to it up to Jesus,
	its name attached itself from within the womb to all the infants.
	It took captive creation and designated it [to be] its own and it ruled on the earth,
	it took their infants [as] tribute [right] from the wombs.
	The crowns from all the nations, thousands of the dead, came to it,
100	families approached and worshipped it with their corpses.
	The first generations were its hostages, and it shut them up,
	so that it might go forth [and] bring even the next ones to be its own.
	The first ones took up the guilt for their posterity,
	and they prepared the way for each one who comes so that he would take up [the guilt] thenceforward.

---

[88] Lit. "maggot."
[89] i.e., Adam.

TEXT AND TRANSLATION

---

⁹⁰ B
⁹¹ B
⁹² CMM₅
⁹³ B
⁹⁴ B
⁹⁵ BM₅
⁹⁶ B
⁹⁷ M
⁹⁸ B
⁹⁹ B

| 105 | Eve cried out with the voice of wailings that death reigned,
all the mouths that saw its yoke on their necks wept.
Lamentations went forth like 'eulogies' concerning its power,
because its victory was sung in all languages.
With miserable weeping it was 'praised' mournfully,
| 110 | And with groans its mightiness was proclaimed.
All the ranks were placed by it [death] under its own,
and all territories henceforth were [underneath it].
For it has not happened that an army would rise up and war with it,
and no one from the earthly ones dared to stand before it.
| 115 | It subdued the world and seized the crowns of all the kings,
and it entered [and] placed them in its power and shut the doors.
It brought them down from that glory of their territories,
and it made them a laughing stock for the worms in the midst of its house.
It seized the [wise] counsels from the wise and stopped them,

---

¹⁰⁰ B
¹⁰¹ B
¹⁰² B

120 and dust filled their mouth so that they would cease from praise.
It deposed the judges and took from them their decrees,
and their thrones fell down to be a footstool for its feet.
It did not condescend to capture [mere] possessions with its bow,
but only over the possessors did it vaunt itself.
125 It despised gold and subdued the lords of riches in its habitation,
instead of properties, it took the property owners[103] to be its bread.[104]
Fearful is its place and he who enters does not get out,
because of this, the righteous feared to quarrel with it.
A memorandum was stretched out and nailed to its door and written thus,
130 "From dust are you, O son of man, and to it will you return."[105]
Everyone coming [into the world] was considered to be a return to Sheol,
and "resurrection" – not even was its story spoken.
Everyone had heard the voice which cries "Let the generations enter."
"Depart from there." was not spoken or announced.[106]

---

[103] "Properties" has to do with what is accomplished through exertion, and "property owners" has to do with those who exert themselves to accomplish something.

[104] Literally, "instead of exertions, it took the exerters (runners)." "Properties," ܩܢܝܢܐ and "property owners," ܩܢܝܐ, sound similar. This stanza continues the idea that death is only interested in people, not what they have, their accomplishments or their wisdom.

[105] Gen. 3:19.

[106] Note the parallel and repetitive structures of lines 133–140: entering vs. departing.

---

[107] M₅
[108] B
[109] B

135 The command went out concerning entering within the grave,
but [concerning] the departure, no one was able to speak about that.
Furthermore, the obedience in this, "you will enter," had become customary,
and it was not heard that "you should obey a voice announcing contrariwise."[110]
Everyone who came, entered, and the door is open to the one who comes,
140 and that a man would depart from within the grave was not considered.

Death, the Victorious King

What city is there that prospered so much as Sheol,
which became rich with harvests without expenses?[111]
What king is there who is so famous like death,
who, being victorious, has not been conquered by another army?
145 Not one of the kings rose up before it to fight,
it humiliated all of them one after another by its might.
It bound Nimrod that mighty hunter,[112]
and it brought in [and] imprisoned the chief of the kings within its[113] darkness.
It utterly destroyed the first crown that Nimrod wore[114] in the land,

---

[110] Lit. "outside."
[111] Lit. "ingatherings without outgoings."
[112] Gen. 10:9.
[113] B.
[114] Lit., "put on."

---

¹¹⁵ M
¹¹⁶ M ; M₅
¹¹⁷ CMM₅
¹¹⁸ M
¹¹⁹ M₅
¹²⁰ CM₅
¹²¹ B
¹²² BM₅
¹²³ B

150   and it buried that first born of primacy with its dust.
From within Babel it began to wrest the crowns of kings,
and it proceeded and went out against the territories of all the nations.
No man sang praises or raised his voice before its authority,
it desolated the land as it exulted without a fight.
155   The upright in generations after generations had stood to speak with it,
they shot at it the arrows of their words and it scorned them.

Enoch Alone Escaped from Death

Enoch was resplendent [and] by his manner of life would conquer death,
he was pleasing[124] and kept pure so that by his uprightness [he would be] the light of his people.
He battled the years with perfection that perchance he [might] subdue it,
160   and he called to the ranks of the beautiful ones to stand with him.
He had plotted[125] and put on righteousness and stood in war,
so that when the arrow of death arrived for him, he would not be pierced by it.
For he had heard[126] that death had reigned over Adam himself,[127]
and he was planning that he would pass from it in safe keeping.

---

[124] Gen. 5:24, Heb. 11:5.
[125] In a positive sense. Perh. 'strategized' given the context.
[126] Pp. followed by ܠ in active sense. See P-S, p. 584.
[127] Lit., "over him, over Adam." Cf. Rom. 5:14.

---

[128] BCMM₅
[129] B
[130] M
[131] B

165 As much as he was able, he was strong in his spiritual beauty,
and he prepared for battle[132] to make a quarrel against death.
And though he was very diligent and raised an army as much as he was able,
unless the place[133] had changed, he was not going to be victorious.
His Lord gave him a hand and He translated[134] him mercifully to Eden,
170 lest he meet with death and it lay hold of him like the rest.
Death pursued him as far as the border [of Eden] and turned from him,
and it did not dare to enter a place that was not its own.
He really had been translated[135] to another place,
for it did not really conquer[136] the valiant one who warred with it.
175 For a little while apprehension came upon death because of this,
lest creation enter in his[137] footsteps to within Paradise.
And although fear entered encouragement also entered [and] took over,
[Death] had bound Adam and Seth and Enosh and shut them up.
It turned again and subdued the corrupt generation with the sword of water,

---

[132] Lit. "extended himself."
[133] ܐܬܪ, see also line 173.
[134] Heb. 11:5.
[135] Heb. 11:5.
[136] Note the infinitive absolute in each line of this stanza.
[137] Enoch's.

165 ܡܛܠ ܕܐܝܟܢ ܗܘܐ ܟܕܢ ܢܥܒܕܝܘܗܝ ܘܢܫܒܠܢܗ܆
ܘܡܣܒܪ ܢܦܫܗ ܘܟܕܘܡܟܠ ܡܕܡܐܐ ܗܘܢܐܐ ܢܚܙܐ.
ܘܟܕ ܠܘܬ ܡܪܗ 138 ܐܬܡܠܝ ܓܝܪ ܡܛܐ ܘܡܢܐ ܗܘܐ.
ܐܝܟ ܐܢܫ ܕܠܐ ܡܬܟ ܗܘܐ ܠܐ ܐܬܐ ܗܘܐ.
ܣܘܕ ܟܕ ܡܢܗ ܐܢܐ ܘܡܢܗ ܚܬܝܣܐܐ ܟܕܢܝ܆
170 ܘܠܐ ܢܗܝܓ ܕܗ ܚܫܘܒܐ 139 ܘܢܚܒܪܘܗܝ ܐܝܟ ܘܚܫܒܐ.
ܘܪܘܓܙܐ ܡܘܢܐ ܚܒܪܐ ܐܝܬܘܗܝ ܐܘܩܝ ܠܘܬܗ.
ܘܠܐ ܐܘܕܥ ܗܘܐ ܘܢܦܩ ܠܕܐܘܢ ܘܟܕ ܡܬܟ ܗܘ.
ܡܥܕܪܢܗ ܐܝܟܢܐ ܗܘܐ ܠܕܐܘܢ ܐܣܪܝܠ.
ܟܕ ܓܝܪ ܡܪܗܛܐ ܪܗܛ ܟܪܘܙܐ ܘܐܡܪܕ ܟܦܪܗ ܀
175 ܡܟܠܐ ܡܢܗ ܡܗܝܡܝܘܗܝ ܗܘܐ ܚܫܘܒܐ ܡܗܓܝܗܘܪܐ.
ܘܠܐ ܐܬܟܠ 140 ܟܕ ܚܙܐܐ ܚܡܝܡܗ ܓܝܪ ܟܘܒܝܫܐ.
ܘܟܕ ܟܠܐ ܘܡܠܐ 141 ܘܟܠܐ ܟܘܬܟܐ ܡܗܡܟܠ ܗܘܐ܆
ܦܩܙܗ ܠܪܘܡ ܘܚܥܝܟ ܘܐܢܗܝ ܘܡܟܝ 142 ܐܢܝ.
ܘܐܘܝ ܐܘܕ ܘܡܥܐ ܟܪܘܙܐ ܡܢܚܠܐ ܚܫܝܩܐ ܘܡܟܢܐ.

---

138 BC ܐܣܪܗ
139 CM ܚܫܘܒܐ
140 CMM₅ ܐܬܟܠ
141 B ܡܠܐ
142 B ܐܘܝ

180   yet it forgot Enoch, a tiny remnant[143] that was left in the land of the living.
He had fled by himself, no others did he lead with himself,
and without companions he alone escaped.

PLEA TO THE HEARER

O hearer do not let the taste of my *memra* lose flavor,
for I did not mingle story with story [just] to talk.
185   I am aiming for the suffering that I had set down at the beginning,
because I did not miss[144] any aspect from the story. [145]

THE BATTLE OF OUR LORD PRIOR TO ENTERING SHEOL

"Concerning the entrance of our Lord to Sheol," I have begun to speak,
and the story demanded of me that it would be spoken in many ways.
It[146] also was urging that we would speak these things which death performed,
190   and what treasures there are in the fortresses which Jesus subdued.
You [O listener] look now at how correct[147] are all my words,
and with understanding let your listening take up the whole story.
Splendid Enoch's battle against death was weak,
and it was not[148] like this one of Jesus who desolated its place.

---

[143] Lit. "seed, grain of corn, atom."

[144] For an ex., see P-S, p. 204, col. b, a).

[145] Mor Jacob "took aim," literally, "bend (the bow)" and he did not "miss" (the target).

[146] Refers to ܐܘܪܚܐ in line 186.

[147] Lit. "straight, upright, honest," or 'orthodox.'

[148] This begins a series of negatives through line 223 where the lines begin with ܠܐ, ܘܠܐ, and ܐܠܐ. It is not possible to begin the lines in English with the negative adverb to give the sense of this Syriac rhetorical feature.

---

[149] B
[150] M
[151] M₅
[152] V continues from this point
[153] V

195 For he[154] did not lay hold of another soul except his own,
and no man would accompany him when he was departing to the land of the living.
He was like Lot, who if he had tarried[155] in the land of Sodom,
he would not have escaped[156] from the conflagration which consumed the town.
And perhaps my brothers in that very manner he hurried and went out,
200 and he himself did not return to see the land that he set off from.
The sound of death was terrifying him, "do not return to your land,"[157]
and he did not turn around lest he fall at the bosom of his mother.
Unlike our Lord Who encountered an opportunity and resisted,
and attacked and was smitten and silent, and was thrust through and disregarded [it].
205 They bound Him and He was silent, they scourged Him and He was calm, they slapped Him and He was radiant,
He suffered at the cross and He did not flee to escape.
He did not desire to go by Himself to the land of the living,
He had entered into the entire captivity so as to take it out like a mighty one.[158]
It was not a great thing that He might be taken up like Elijah,[159]

---

[154] i.e., Enoch.
[155] For the conditional clause translation, see Noeldeke, para. 375, p. 311.
[156] For ܩܠܛ, see Gen. 19:17–21.
[157] Gen. 19:21.
[158] ܐܝܟ ܚܣܝܢܐ. See line 247 for the same phrase.
[159] II Ki. 2:11.

---

[160] B
[161] C
[162] B

210   it was nothing for Him to be translated in the manner of Enoch.[163]
He did not elude[164] death as indeed did these,
because He had desired to go up to the place of His Father along with the multitudes.
He was smitten from the front [and] not from behind was He pierced,
because this too is found only among warriors.
215   He did not turn His back to the arrows from the pursuers,
because He opposed [them] with His hands like a brave man and did not preserve Himself.
He directed His face against the shameless spit,
and He did not turn His back[165] to the shame that befell Him.
And to show the power of His love, He endured so much,
220   through Isaiah[166] He wrote [and] announced to us these things which He bore.
"Neither from shame nor from spit did I turn My face,
and I stretched My hands all day so that I might bear the sufferings."
He did not fear nor flee like a faint-hearted man who deserts the ranks,
He bore beatings that he might restore the spoil that death had laid hold of.

---

[163] Heb. 11:5.
[164] Lit. "show the back to."
[165] Lit. "turn his neck." Cf. line 215.
[166] Is. ch. 52–53.

---

[167] B
[168] B

The Lord's Vision of Sheol

225 He had seen this ruler of darkness who spoiled the earth,
as well as all the generations, one after another, coming into his hands.
He saw the city of Sheol opened, and [all] races entering [it],
and He undertook His journey so that He, too, would enter [it] bodily.
The just entered and did not go out again to the land they had left,
230 the righteous went down and did not go up from it because it covered up everyone.
The prisoners who were within were never helped by anything from a man,
and it shut up there everyone who entered just like his companions.
The captives are shut up and there is no door that opens for them[169] to leave,
and it utterly destroys everyone who showed up to enter after his head.[170]
235 Noah entered to its place[171] and it bound him there and Shem with him,
Abraham entered and he could not help the captives.[172]
Isaac had entered and was added to the number [there],
and his son Jacob, even him did it thrust back among the darkened ones.
Moses the deliverer rose up in Egypt and lead out the People,

---

[169] 3 p. s. f. impf. To agree with collective noun, ܐܣܝܪܐ.
[170] i.e., Adam.
[171] Ms. B: "just Noah entered."
[172] Perhaps a reference to captives of Sodom, Gen. 14:13–18.

---

173 B
174 B
175 C
176 B
177 C add.
178 C
179 BV
180 B
181 M
182 B
183 M
184 B

240   yet he was unable to lead out Sheol's prisoners.
Joshua had overthrown high walls and slaughtered kings,
but when he had entered the city of death, he did not depart from it.
Furthermore, David killed that mighty warrior of the Philistines,
he was illustrious in battle, yet death imprisoned him just like his companions.
245   And though the entrants into the doors of Sheol thus multiplied,
yet there was not a foot that could depart from it to the place of the living.
Then our Lord, like a mighty one[185] prepared Himself,
to enter and prepare the way of peace in [that] fearful place.
He had seen the place that no man enters unless he had died,
250   and He desired[186] to die to enter [and] take captive the captivity[187] of death.

THE INCARNATION

And because it was not easy for Him to taste death spiritually,
He became a man[188] so that He might be mortal and desolate Sheol.
He was clothed with a body from that very family which was being led captive,
and in the likeness of a captive, He entered the city while subduing it.

---

[185] Cf. line 208.
[186] Jo. 10:17.
[187] Eph. 4:7.
[188] اِحَدٍ.

---

189 C
190 B
191 C add.
192 MM₅
193 BV
194 B

255 He did not fly [away like a bird], but entered like Gabriel to Daniel,
and He did not fly around but descended like Michael to the Hebrews.
A silent corpse that could be touched, entered Sheol,
[just] like the very figure[195] in which every man enters at that door.
He was clothed with the likeness of the region so that He might walk in the region of death,[196]
260 and in humiliation see the walls of the great walled city.
He had gone by Himself so that He might preach His Good News to the departed ones,
and by His footsteps He might prepare the way to the region of the living.

THE LORD'S JOURNEY IN SHEOL

He had wrapped Himself with the shroud of the dead as He was entering,
and in the linen garments and the body that He was clothed with, they brought [and] placed Him.
265 He entered quietly and explored the place silently,
He went around in Sheol three days, and He spied out its depths.
He had seen the world that was laid waste and cast down without pity,
and the captives piled up in heaps in the land of death.
He had seen heaps[197] of men without number,

---

[195] ܛܘܦܣܐ (τυπος)

[196] Note the play on words due to the similarity of the first and last words of the line: ܐܬܪܐ...ܕܐܬܪܐ.

[197] ܝܓܪܐ – refers to heap of stones. Cf. Gen. 31:47.

---

[198] B
[199] M
[200] B
[201] BV

270   and the skeletons of the just which had become dust in Sheol.
Wisely did He enter the place according to His attire,
so that quietly He might see the ambushes made for Him.
He had been concealed as He was entering through the doors of death,
so that suddenly he might cast amazement on the captor.
275   The King of life was clothed and altered in the likeness of the dead,
so that as a citizen He might see the place and its secrets.
David had seen Him as He was coming to enter Sheol,
and he ran to open the door before Him with his songs.
He took up his lyre and began to play among the departed ones,
280   and in allegories tell them the good news concerning the Son of his Lord.
He raised a cry and death heard and its knees knocked together,
as he was saying, "behold the Freeman dwells among the dead!"
He pointed out to death that the Dead One is alive – this One who came!
He really deceived[202] you [so that] He could enter [and] desolate all your place!

---

[202] Infinitive absolute.

---

²⁰³ M
²⁰⁴ P starts from this point
²⁰⁵ P
²⁰⁶ BV
²⁰⁷ B
²⁰⁸ P
²⁰⁹ B
²¹⁰ P
²¹¹ P
²¹² P
²¹³ P

285 You should not rejoice over Him Who came into your hands and
dwells with you,
in order to lay you waste, He entered without force [and] your
bow captured Him.
Read in the Scriptures and see that He is not of your number,
for He is a Freeman and by His volition[214] He took your yoke.
Because He seeks to destroy you and because of this He was
willing and you bound Him,
290 He was your Guest, and at His departure your dwelling becomes
desolate.
He is not from the servants; you may not deride Him who re-
clines in your house,
for His mortality is by His volition,[215] and He is not subject to
you.
Behold the Freeman entered the house of the dead[216] and slept
there,
so that He might make a deliverance for the bondage of the race
of the dead!

Comparison with Jonah

295 He had descended to the depth like Bar Mattai[217] to the bottom
of the sea,
and death received Him like the great fish [received] Jonah.
His entrance within the grave also resembled,
that descent of the son of the Hebrews within the sea.[218]
Dead Jonah was made alive in the bowels of the fish,

---

[214] Jo. 10:17.
[215] Jo. 10:17.
[216] i.e., the grave or Sheol.
[217] Jonah is the son of Matti. See Jonah 1:1 in the Peshitta.
[218] Note Mor Jacob's distinction between "entrance," ܡܥܠܐ, in the title of this homily, and "descent," ܡܚܬܐ.

285 لَا اَسِبَرا كَه وَاِاِا لَاِتَّىپ هَعِرَا[219] حَهُاُمِ:
---

[219] B
[220] BPV

300   he was buried though living – suffocating and praying,
        imprisoned and supplicating.
Hidden and speaking, he was cast into destruction, forsaken in
        the abyss [of the sea],
bound up in the waves and whispering there at the base of the
        mountains.
The bars of the place are locked in his face in the heart of the
        seas,
death carries him and it bore him like [it bore] his Lord.
305   Our Lord had given this sign to the sons of His People,
and it suffices to persuade [them] that even His mortality was
        vitality.

THE DEAD ONE GIVES LIFE

In this form He had descended alive to the swamp of the dead:
killed, yet raising [to life]; a departed one in Sheol, yet laying it
        waste.
[It is] a wonder to speak, because death is conquered by the
        Dead One,
310   and the Silent Buried One subdues the region of the house of the
darkened ones.
He had entered to make peace there in the desert of Sheol,
and in that waste, the cries of life would be celebrated.
He had gone down to prepare a clear path in the fearful valley,
so that everyone might travel without fear to the place of life.[221]

---

[221] In contrast to Sheol, the place of the dead.

---

²²² B
²²³ CMP
²²⁴ BV
²²⁵ M
²²⁶ P
²²⁷ MV
²²⁸ B

315 He had journeyed in the depths in which all the merchants were despoiled,
and there He hunted the robber who plundered the earth.
He entered so that He might search out the burial caves[229] from [among] the spoils,[230]
and he carried and brought out all sorts [of spoils] that death had snatched.
He went down to pacify the desolate waste with the bands of the Watchers,
320 and that the place full of terrors might resound with the angels.
There the crowds [of the departed] thronged the crowds of the heavenly ones,
the legions gathered and the armies were in formation and the ranks sang praises.

Comparison with the Patriarch Jacob

Jacob had slept on the top of the mountain as he depicted it,
and the host of heaven descended to him with great praise.[231]
325 And if it happened that the angels descended to where the servant slept,
how much more would they have descended there to where their Lord had slept?
And if the watchers honored their companion in the place where he slept,
would they not indeed have descended to their Lord to where He slept?
Even Jacob himself who slept in Bethel when he was fleeing,

---

[229] Lit., "caves of the graves."
[230] i.e., the dead.
[231] Gen. 28:12.

---

²³² P
²³³ BCMM₅PV
²³⁴ V |
²³⁵ P
²³⁶ P |
²³⁷ P |
²³⁸ CMM₅PV
²³⁹ B
²⁴⁰ M
²⁴¹ B |

330   had depicted the death of the Son by his sleeping on the top of the mountain.
He set a stone only [as] his pillows, and the upright one slept,
as our Lord also [slept] – the ground of the grave became His bed.
He was crucified in his sleep, as if in death, with a staff in his hand,
he had depicted there exactly the crucifixion of the Son.
335   He embraced his[242] staff and he held [it] in sleep as if in death,
in all of it, he had truly depicted the crucifixion and the passion.
The watchers honored the foreshadowing of the Son of God,
the angels descended because of the symbol they saw there.
And if there was honor from the exalted ones for the figure,
340   [then] the hosts [of heaven] were insignificant [compared] to the True One Himself.
And if the ladder[243] was erected on the mountain on account of Jacob,
[then] heaven is insignificant [compared] to the grave below on account of Jesus.

Christ's Death and the Overthrow of Sheol

Through the descent of our Lord, this peace was in Sheol itself,
and praise resounded in the desolate place of the house of the departed ones.

---

[242] Mss. BPV.
[243] Gen. 28:12.

---

²⁴⁴ P
²⁴⁵ BCMM₅PV
²⁴⁶ M₅
²⁴⁷ BPV
²⁴⁸ M
²⁴⁹ M
²⁵⁰ P om.
²⁵¹ B ; P om.; V
²⁵² M₅P ; P add.

345   The host of heaven descended [and] entered into the place of death,
and the doors of Sheol began shaking on account of the exalted ones.
The city of strength that had not been subdued by mighty warriors,
into it the Slain One entered, and He broke it down suddenly and it became a laughing stock.
The King is asleep[253] yet the fortress which is more rebellious than any is subdued,

350   He was bound in sleep yet He freed the prisoners so that they would go out with Him.
Humbly did He enter through the door all by Himself,
so that He might free the prisoners and take the bars[254] [of Sheol] and bring out the people.
And although like a dead man He had entered and lay hidden inside the door,
He began, by His power, to break down the walls of that 'place of pleasure.'

355   He stirred in death itself as also Jonah [stirred] in the bowels of the fish,
which carried him and swam in the depths of the sea as it went about.
He proceeded in the deep for three days in the belly of death,
He had descended and arrived in the heart of the earth so that He might bring up Adam.
He had plunged[255] into death so that from within the depth He might draw up our race,

---

[253] As in death.

[254] ܡܘܟܠܐ

[255] A play on ܥܡܕ; alternatively, "was baptized in death." Cf. Mk. 10:39, Rom. 6:3.

TEXT AND TRANSLATION   63

---

²⁵⁶ P |
²⁵⁷ P ,
²⁵⁸ C ; M
²⁵⁹ BM₅V ; P
²⁶⁰ M |
²⁶¹ B
²⁶² P
²⁶³ B
²⁶⁴ B
²⁶⁵ P
²⁶⁶ M

360 He explored Sheol to take up the riches which were swallowed up by it.
He had entered so that He might bring out the treasures which death had amassed in its cave,
and to empty the walled city that gathered the spoil of the all the earth.[267]
He entered the garners which[268] are only touched in death,
He had travelled in the place that none but the slain [can] see it.[269]

365 He had lodged in the place that none but the buried [can] dwell in it,
He entered the ambushes that are experienced[270] by none but the dead.[271]
He had travelled and came forth[272] right up to the limit of corruption,[273]
but He did not enter, and it[274] saw that He had returned in health.
For He had subdued the entire place gallantly,

370 and it[275] could not compel [Him] to see corruption like a frail [person].

---

[267] Cf. ܐܠܘ in P.
[268] Note the use of ܠܐ, followed by ܠܐ plus the participle in the consecutive lines, 364–366. On the use of ܠܐ, see Noldeke, pp. 307–309, esp. 309.
[269] Cf. line 249.
[270] Lit., "known."
[271] Note the multiple parallels between lines 363 and 364, not only in grammatical structure but also in words. There is also a rhetorical structure of a b b* a*.
[272] Ms. B reads, ܡܛܐ, "reached."
[273] Cf. Ps. 16:10, Acts 2:27, 31; 13:34,35.
[274] i.e., death.
[275] i.e., Sheol.

TEXT AND TRANSLATION

---

[276] BCMM₅PV
[277] B
[278] P
[279] MP
[280] B
[281] B ; P
[282] B
[283] P
[284] B

Conclusion

He conquered death and took its crown and uprooted its wall,
He subdued the walled city and took out the spoil and broke
    down its walls.
He entered like a despised one and He tricked death and turned
    around [and] bound it.
Blessed is the Watchful One Who slept in Sheol so that He might
    awaken[285] Adam!

The end of
"Concerning the Entrance of our Lord into Sheol"

---

[285] "Awaken" and "Watchful One" have the same root, ܥܝܪ.

---

²⁸⁶ B ܩܕܩܙ

²⁸⁷ B ܘܩܝܗ

²⁸⁸ BCMM₅PV ܠܩܩܣ

²⁸⁹ B ܕܪܐܗ

²⁹⁰ CM₅ ܩܐܘܝܟܡ

²⁹¹ P ܘܩܩܝܟܗ

BIBLIOGRAPHY

Akhrass, Severios Roger, and Daniel L. McConaughy, "Ṣemaḥ, *Anatole*, and *Denḥa*: Translation and Evolution of a Messianic Title," *Syriac Orthodox Patriarchal Journal* 60 (2022), pp. 1–18.

Akhrass, Roger, and Imad Syryany, *160 Unpublished Homilies of Jacob of Serugh*, 2 vols., Damascus: Department of Syriac Studies – Syriac Orthodox Patriarchate, 2017.

Bedjan, Paul, *Homiliae Selectae Mar-Jacobi Sarugensis*, I–V, Lipzig: Otto Harrassowitz (1905–10). Reprint, Gorgias Press, 2006.

Brock, Sebastian P., "The Gates/Bars of Sheol Revisited," *Sayings of Jesus: Canonical and Non-canonical: Essays in Honour of T.Baarda*, ed. By W. L. Peterson, J.S, Vos and H. J. de Jong, Supplements to Novum Testamentum, vol. 89 (1997), pp. 7–24.

Brock, Sebastian, "Yaʿqub of Serugh (ca. 451–521) [Syr. Orth.]," *Gorgias Encyclopedic Dictionary of the Syriac Heritage Electronic Edition*: https://gedsh.bethmardutho.org/entry/Yaqub-of-Serugh.

McConaughy, Daniel, and Jacob Thekeparampil, *The Homily of Mor Jacob Concerning the Star that Appeared to the Magi*, Awṣar Ṣlawoto 11, Kottayam: SEERI, 2024.

Noldeke, Theodor, *Compendious Syriac Grammar*, Trans. James A. Chrichton, reprint Winona Lake: Eisenbrauns, 2001. ("Noldeke").

Payne Smith, Jessie, *A Compendious Syriac Dictionary*, Oxford: Clarendon Press, 1976. ("P-S")

Sokoloff, Michael, A Syriac Lexicon, Winona Lake, IN: Eisenbrauns, 2009.

Jacob Thekeparambil and Daniel McConaughy, *Jacob of Serugh's Three Mimre on Simon Peter: 1. On the Question of our Lord and the Revelation Simon Received from the Father, 2. On Simon Kepha When Our Lord Said "Get Behind Me Satan," 3. On the Denial of Simon,* Awṣar Ṣlawoto 10, Kottayam: SEERI, 2023.

Thekeparambil, Jacob, and Daniel McConaughy, "The Star and the Magi in Jacob of Serugh and the Early Syriac Tradition," *Syriac Orthodox Patriarchal Journal* 59, (2021), pp. 41–54.

INDEX

References are to line number.

TOPICAL INDEX

Abraham   236
Adam   93, 163, 178, 358, 374
Ambush   32, 272, 366
Angel   320, 325, 338
Army   82, 113, 144, 167
Bars   17, 303, 353
Battle   159, 166, 193, 244
Body   253, 264
Captive, Captor   97, 123, 209, 233, 236, 250, 253, 254, 268, 275, 286
Cave   317, 361
City   25, 68, 71, 141, 227, 242, 254, 260, 347, 362, 372
Clothed   253, 259, 264, 275
Corrupt, Corruption   179, 367, 370
Cross   5, 35, 47, 60, 207
Daniel   255
Darkness, Darkness   147, 225, 238, 310
David   243, 277

Dawn   2, 3
Dead   3, 6, 63, 75, 77, 99, 263, 275, 282, 283, 293, 294, 299, 307, 309, 353, 366
Death   42, 48, 49, 50, 51, 52, 53, 56, 75, 85, 105, 111, 143, 157, 162, 163, 165, 170, 171, 175, 178, 189, 193, 201, 212, 224, 242, 244, 250, 251, 259, 268, 273, 281, 283, 296, 304, 309, 318, 330, 333, 335, 345, 355, 357, 359, 361, 363, 371, 373
Deep   357
Depth   1, 266, 295, 315, 355, 359
Descend   58, 254, 295, 307, 324, 325, 326, 328, 338, 345, 358
Die   5, 249, 250
Door   12, 73, 89, 116, 129, 139, 233, 245, 258, 273, 278, 346, 351, 353

Earth   65, 70, 97, 114, 225, 316, 358, 362
Eden   169, 171
Elijah   210
Enoch   157, 180, 193, 211
Enosh   178
Enter   12, 18, 19, 23, 36, 68, 72, 79, 83, 116, 127, 133, 135, 137, 139, 172, 176, 177, 209, 227, 228, 229, 232, 234, 235, 236, 237, 242, 248, 249, 250, 254, 255, 257, 258, 263, 265, 271, 273, 277, 284, 286, 293, 311, 317, 345, 348, 351, 353, 361, 366, 368, 373
Figure   258, 339
Fortress   70, 190, 349
Fortress   70, 190, 349
Gabriel   255
Gate   16
Grave   20, 135, 140, 297, 332, 342
Heaven   321, 324, 340, 342, 345
Immortal   5
Immortal   5
Issac   237
Jacob   238, 323, 329, 341
Jesus   95, 190, 194, 342
Jonah   296, 299, 355
Joshua   239
Kill   50, 67, 243, 308
King   9, 21, 45, 57, 67, 87, 115, 143, 145, 148, 151, 241, 275, 349

King, Kingdom   9, 21, 45, 57, 67, 87, 115, 143, 145, 148, 151, 241, 275, 349
Life   7, 8, 157, 275, 308, 312, 314
Michael   256
Mind   4, 10, 13, 22, 25, 37
Moses   239
Murder   7, 8
Noah   235
Paradise   176
Prison, Prisoner   148, 231, 240, 244, 300, 350, 357
Rank   25, 28, 111, 160, 223, 322
Seth   178
Sheol   1, 48, 64, 69, 77, 89, 131, 141, 187, 227, 240, 245, 257, 266, 270, 277, 308, 311, 343, 346, 352, 360, 374
Shroud   263
Sign   41, 305
Sleep   330, 333, 335, 349, 350
Slept   293, 323, 325, 326, 327, 329, 330, 331, 332, 374
Son   130, 238, 280, 298, 305, 330, 334, 337
Suffer, Suffering   12, 26, 41, 50, 52, 53, 60, 185, 205, 222
Sun   3
Symbol   338

Wall 35, 42, 64, 68, 241, 260, 354, 360, 362, 371, 372

War 113, 161, 174
Warrier 214, 243, 347
Watcher 319, 327, 337

INDEX OF SCRIPTURAL ALLUSIONS

Genesis
- 3:19   130
- 5:24   158
- 10:9   147
- 14:13–18   236
- 19:21   201
- 19:17–21   198
- 28:12   324
- 28:12   341
- 31:47   269

2 Kings
- 2:11   210

Psalms
- 16:10   367

Proverbs
- 30:15–16   71

Habakkuk
- 2:5   71

Matthew
- 6:12   22
- 10:39   359
- 26:39   51
- 26:42   51

John
- 10:17   250, 288, 292

Acts
- 2:27   367
- 2:31   367
- 13:34–35   367

Romans
- 5:14   164
- 6:3   359

Ephesians
- 4:7   250

Colossians
- 2:20   6

Hebrews
- 1:1   1
- 11:5   158, 169, 173, 211

www.ingramcontent.com/pod-product-compliance
Lightning Source LLC
Chambersburg PA
CBHW052135300426
44116CB00010B/1915